How to THRIVE in REMOTE WORKING ENVIRONMENTS

Ryan Fahey

© Copyright 2021 Ryan B Fahey

All rights reserved. No part of this publication may be reproduced, distributed, or transmitted in any form or by any means, including photocopying, recording, or other electronic or mechanical methods, without the prior written permission of the publisher, except in the case of brief quotations embodied in critical reviews and certain other noncommercial uses permitted by copyright law.

Although the author and publisher have made every effort to ensure that the information in this book was correct at press time, the author and publisher do not assume and hereby disclaim any liability to any party for any loss, damage, or disruption caused by errors or omissions, whether such errors or omissions result from negligence, accident, or any other cause.

Adherence to all applicable laws and regulations, including international, federal, state and local governing professional licensing, business practices, advertising, and all other aspects of doing business in the US, Canada or any other jurisdiction is the sole responsibility of the reader and consumer.

Neither the author nor the publisher assumes any responsibility or liability whatsoever on behalf of the consumer or reader of this material. Any perceived slight of any individual or organization is purely unintentional.

The resources in this book are provided for informational purposes only and should not be used to replace the specialized training and professional judgment of a health care or mental health care professional.

Neither the author nor the publisher can be held responsible for the use of the information provided within this book. Please always consult a trained professional before making any decision regarding the treatment of yourself or others.

For more information, email faheyconsulting@gmail.com.
ISBN: 9781777686109

CONTENTS

ACKNOWLEDGEMENTS 5
FOREWORD 7
INTRODUCTION 9

Chapter 1 13
**A 2,000-YEAR-OLD BRAIN IN
A LIGHTNING SPEED SOCIETY** 13

Chapter 2 21
YOUR ENERGY AUDIT 21

Chapter 3 31
ADDING VALUE IS ENOUGH 31
CREATE AN ACCOMPLISHMENTS SPREADSHEET 33
BREATHE LIFE INTO YOUR JOURNAL, DAILY 35
**PLAN A QUARTERLY ASSESSMENT
AND REFLECTION PERIOD** 36
**SEEK OUT MOMENTS EACH DAY WHERE
YOU FEEL YOU CAN ADD VALUE** 38
PLAN TO ADD VALUE 39
SET A CALENDAR PROMPT (*DID I ADD VALUE TODAY?*) 40

Chapter 4 41
OVERCOMING IMPOSTER SYNDROME 41
SEEK OUT A MENTOR 47
GET CLEAR AND SIMPLE WITH EACH TASK 48
OWN YOUR WORD 50
TAKE OWNERSHIP 50
FIND SMALL WINS 51

Chapter 5 53
DEVELOPING YOUR EQ OVER YOUR IQ 53

Chapter 6 61
ROUTINE IS EVERYTHING 61

Chapter 7 67
SWAPPING DISTRACTIONS 67
A SINGULAR WORK SPACE 72

Chapter 8 75
MATURING WITH REMOTE WORK 75

Chapter 9 81
THE NEW SKILLS NEEDED FOR REMOTE WORK 81
#1 BEING HUMAN AND STAYING CREATIVE 82
#2 STAYING SELF-DISCIPLINED 84
#3 BUILDING BOUNDARIES 85
#4 STAYING SOCIAL 86
#5 THE ABILITY TO HYPERFOCUS 88
#6 CREATE SCIENCE EXPERIMENTS 89
#7 IDEATION & EXECUTION 90

Chapter 10 93
REMOTIVATION 93
JOURNALING 94
RECORDING MONTHLY MILESTONES 95

Chapter 11 99
SELF-CARE 99
CONCLUSION 103
NOTES 105

BOOK RECOMMENDATIONS FOR REMOTE WORKERS 109

ACKNOWLEDGEMENTS

This book would not have been possible without the support of my incredible wife, Amber. Walking side by side with her has given me the space to write this book for you. Without her encouragement, support, and unwavering belief in me as a writer, this book would not have been possible.

I also want to thank my talented Editor, Kristine Johnston, for helping me take this book from good to great.

This book was originally written on the ancestral territory of the Mi'kma'ki people (Nova Scotia), with final edits and publication on the traditional unceded territory of the Algonquin Anishnaabeg People (Ottawa).

FOREWORD

In March of 2020, my family and I had just returned home to Montreal after a restful vacation in South Carolina. During our stay, I was proud of the daily routine I had built for myself: I'd wake up early in the morning (around 5:00 AM), complete a strength-based workout or yoga session, and then get some important work done while eating breakfast. I remember feeling both proud and excited that I had the discipline and capacity to continue to work on important projects despite working remotely from an Airbnb in a different country.

As soon as we got back to Quebec, the global COVID-19 pandemic went from being a story on the news to an event that would shape the rest of our lives. My wife and I are both teachers and we suddenly found ourselves having to scramble as our schools switched to a remote learning reality. Our home had morphed into a combination of both workplace and daycare as we struggled to balance raising our son, completing our teacher duties, and trying to stay healthy and safe.

The dream of being a remote worker had now turned into a nightmare situation that had forced us to go into survival mode.

Our healthy habits went out the window, any sense of balance that we had cultivated as a family was crumbling a part, and we found ourselves feeling utterly overwhelmed by the demands that the world was now placing on us.

As an entrepreneur, the hit to my productivity and confidence during this time was significant. Despite having invested in systems that would allow me to build my side business while working as a full-time teacher over the years, I suddenly found myself scrambling to get work done, struggling with imposter syndrome, and wondering how I could continue to add value to the lives of others through my work in a world that now felt more isolated than ever.

Over time, I was able to find my footing and gain some clarity in regard to navigating this new reality of ours. That said, that success only came after months of lost productivity and feeling "stuck".

Ryan's book provides readers with tips, tools, and tactics that can help you overcome such feelings on a much shorter timeline so that you can get back to feeling like yourself, feeling confident in your work, and feeling like you can thrive despite these sudden changes in your professional and personal lives. The strategies he shares are simple, effective, and easy to implement right away so that you can start experiencing those early wins, build momentum, and regain control of your work and of your life.

No matter your background, experience, or comfort level with remote work, there is advice in these pages that will serve you well and that can help you get out of those moments of feeling "stuck". I wish I had been able to read this book earlier!

Joey Feith
Montreal, Canada
March 15, 2021

INTRODUCTION

How can we thrive in remote working environments?

This question prompted the initial discovery of this book.

In 2020, the world was thrown into a global pandemic. While I could have written an entire book on pandemic life itself, I choose instead to write about one of the disruptions that the pandemic caused in the workforce. Workplaces across the globe that were not necessarily early adopters of remote work were literally thrown into that category overnight. Our professional world changed forever.

Many of us muddled our way through the chaotic transition to this new way of working and somehow came out the other side. However, during that process, we did not have the time to step back and assess our remote working conditions to really understand what would be needed within our internal remote systems to thrive in our forward-facing remote jobs. Sure, we may have scanned articles in journals like *Thrive Journal* or digital papers like the *Huffington Post*, but did we actually stop, pause, and reflect on what the heck was happening to us? Yes, we swapped the khakis for robes and the dresses for pajamas, but those are short-term, comfortable changes. How did we address the longer-term changes impacting our work lives?

This book is about the internal. It is about internal systems, routines, decisions, reflections, and manifestations that can lead you down a career of sustainable work in remote settings **without compromising your sanity, performance, or wellbeing.**

Our world is moving faster than ever, causing us to constantly adapt, think, react, and sometimes scramble, for the "right" answer, the "right" decision to make. And with this pace unfolding faster and faster in remote settings, we must stop to master ourselves as we transition from traditional to remote office environments.

This is why feelings of loneliness and isolation are at an all-time high and why this thing called "imposter syndrome" continues to rear its ugly head in places it should never have been in the first place. This is why the word "burnout" was the most searched word of the year in 2019 according to *Thrive Journal*.[1]

So what does all of this mean for you and I?

1. Should we settle in for the long winter nap of remote working and call it a day?
2. Are our pajama bottoms from 9-5 here to stay?
3. Are we set on a course for long-term remote work without a clear way?
4. If working remotely, how can we create a system that allows us to thrive each day?

The answer to these questions, as well as many others, lives within the pages of this book. So, grab your favorite coffee cup and pair of warm socks and get ready to laugh, cry, and discover new ways of approaching your work so you can thrive in your remote working environment for years to come!

Chapter 1

A 2,000-YEAR-OLD BRAIN IN A LIGHTNING SPEED SOCIETY

"You just do the best you can with what you've got... and sometimes magic strikes."
-Sally Field

In attempting to understand what is needed to thrive in remote working environments, we first have to take a giant step back. *In looking back, we may in fact be able to look forward.*

As humans, we have been around for centuries, slowly evolving and slowly creating a better world through passion and vocation.

I've often thought about how cool it would have been to be the first person who created fire; about how much attention and thought really went into that. I'm curious if someone discovered it and then learned how to harness it and recreate it in controlled settings. I wonder how long this took, too. I doubt it was instantaneous. It was likely thought about over days, weeks, or even years until the conditions aligned for that thinking to be applied to igniting a fire.

I've also thought about how fascinating it would have been to be the first person to see the moon on a clear evening. The purity of that moment for that individual must have been absolutely romantic. To look up and realize that there is something beyond the ocean, the land around us, and the sky above us must have been an incredibly enlightening moment. I imagine this happened thousands of years ago. Yet, it took at least 1,950+ years to finally send someone to the surface of the moon and to prove that it was indeed what we had been looking at as humans for thousands of years.

1,950+ years!

That's a long time to make something happen.

Fast forward to the 1900s. How many astronauts do you think humanity sent to the moon between 1968 and 1972? Well, according to NASA, 24 made the voyage from America alone.[2]

Think about this for a moment. Between when the first person looked up and saw the moon, until the late 1960s, we spent countless years learning, studying, and forming ideas about the moon. Then, within just about a half-decade, 24 astronauts landed on it. If we use this as a microcosm of how the pace of innovation, technology, and humanity has shifted in the past century, it is absolutely astonishing. With this rapid pace of innovation, we haven't taken a moment to stop, pause, and reflect on what the byproduct is of this pace on our brains and what this means for our day-to-day work.

Let's use Apple as another example. In 1985, Steve Jobs declared that computers would be essential in most homes.[3] Some 30+ years later, he turned out to be right. It did not take over

1,900 years for this change to happen. It did not take thousands of years for people to make the decision to buy a computer for their home. This idea was thought into action and on the market in less than two decades.

Now, what does the birth of fire, 24 American voyages to the moon, and a declaration from Steve Jobs in 1985 have in common? These are three examples of how the pace of human innovation has continued to evolve faster and faster.

1. So, what about our brains?
2. Are they evolving too? And, if so, are they evolving fast enough to keep up with innovation and the pace of our current society?
3. What does this mean for our work?

So many questions to answer!

In neuroscience, there is a term called "cognitive pruning" that describes when new habits, experiences, and actions begin forming new cognitive pathways while trimming older neural pathways. Simply put, this process allows our brains to stay efficient *and* effective, and to keep up with innovation.[4] Much of the research indicates that pruning occurs even into our late 20s, but I suggest that this continues into our 30s as well. Not because it should, but because it needs to.

This is why, as we mature, we tend to forget many of our childhood experiences. This is why we change as we mature from teenagers to adults. Even right now, your brain is likely pruning something old for something new to help you keep up with new information. This is a fantastic thing! Pruning can enable us to keep up with the changes that are happening in and around our lives. But is it enough? Can we continue to keep up with the rapid pace of innovation and information coming at us? Can we continue to keep up as pruning slows down with age but the pace of change remains faster than ever?

While I will list some book recommendations at the back of this book to help you dive deeper into your 2,000-year-old brain's capacity, for now, let's do a short exercise.

> **Step 1: Write down the names of the closest three people in your life**
>
> **Step 2: Without looking it up, write down their full phone number**

My guess is that you likely wrote down one or two of those numbers but couldn't recall all three off the top of your head. Why is this?

Well, let me first say that this is not because you don't care about them. This is a consequence of the neurobiological process of cognitive pruning.

I remember as a child opening the cupboard and seeing the handwritten list of phone numbers. I remember the day I had to learn those phone numbers in case of emergency. Now, like most of you, I have a smartphone that does everything I need - it not only stores those important numbers but remembers them for me. It calls people for me, sends messages for me, and I hardly need to physically dial a number at all anymore. I just find their name and hit "call" while my phone does the rest.

This is one of the main reasons why we can no longer recall the phone numbers of the three people closest to us. Because we don't need to remember.

So, we know that our brains are able to adapt to change. This is great news. However, I'll ask again, is it enough? Are we able to continue to keep pace with how much is being thrown at us? Will we pass the point of no return, or reach a place where the pace of innovation and information moves so fast we can't keep up? Is this already happening?

I believe it is.

I believe that we live in a lightning speed society with a 2,000-year-old brain that is trying desperately to keep up.

In 2012, it seemed like the average amount of time a specific topic was considered "trending" on Twitter was almost double what it is today. In fact, by the time you finish reading this chapter, trending topics may have already shifted.

What does this mean? It means that more topics, voices, and communication around those topics and voices are moving at least 2x faster than just a few years ago.

In the sporting world, I remember the days when you would wake up in the morning with anticipation, excited to get the sports highlights from the night before. Now, sports broadcasting stations are live-tweeting and posting immediate updates for their subscribers and followers so that they know the outcome of a particular game instantly. Before you can even take a moment to process how the game went, by scrolling through a series of highlights, you are given the immediate outcome.

Here is another example of the speed of information from Think with Google:

*"Pick a query, any query. 'Weather, New York City.' 'Nineteenth-century Russian literature.' 'When is the 2012 Super Bowl?' Now type it into a Google search box. As you type, we predict the rest of your query, comb through billions of web pages, rank the sites, images, videos, and products we find, and present you with the very best results. **The entire process takes, in many cases, less than a tenth of a second – it's practically instant.**"* - Urs Hoelzle[5]

So, where does this leave us?

I believe that without the proper support, strategies, knowledge, and understanding, it puts us into an existential crisis of interest and attention. If we cannot manage the level of information that is coming at us, how can we possibly find the day-to-day mental space to thrive? Simply put, what we put our attention towards, grows.

This brings me back to the question about our work and how that has changed and will continue to change into the future. With more and more of the global workforce entering or transitioning to remote work in the 2020s, how can we possibly thrive in remote settings with this 2,000-year-old brain?

If we cannot control how much we are able to process and when, our brains, as well as our bodies, will only ever remain in survival mode and won't be capable of thriving in any environment, let alone remote working ones. This is why this book is mostly focused on "the how" around thriving and "the where" in a remote working environment.

While most of society will live in this state of constant processing, chaos, and information overload, this book is about how we are going to use this 2,000-year-old brain, along with our bodies to our competitive advantage, so that we can move beyond surviving to thriving in our remote working environments.

Knowing that the conditions all around us are incubators for distraction, exhaustion, burnout, loneliness, isolation, and confusion, I am going to take the opportunity in these next chapters to share strategies that will allow you to thrive in the new world you are working in. *It is my aim to show you how to protect your attention while building your confidence through investing in your wellbeing to produce a sustainable, successful life as a remote worker.*

Consider the following chapters to be your personal "thrivability blueprint," which will allow you to remain focused, clear, and in tune with your wellbeing as you journey to thrive in your remote working environment, forever.

Chapter 2

YOUR ENERGY AUDIT

"You are never too old to set another goal or to dream a new dream."
-Les Brown

One of the most important parts of uncovering the hidden conditions that are essential to thriving in remote working environments is the act of looking inward, critically, in the form of an internal energy audit.

In business, we have an auditing process that keeps the business moving forward. This process often reveals areas that need to be shored up and other areas that could be further explored, all while keeping the business accountable. Why should our lives be any different?

Completing an energy audit in your own life can unveil many things. Most importantly, it can show us where and how we are spending our energy and how we can shift our energy to improve our lives.

When we look inward and reflect on where our energy goes each day, it can tell us a lot about whether and how we can thrive in the 2020s.

In a world that demands our full attention, presence, and focus, our energy is often the first area to degrade when our cup isn't full. Think about it - when was the last time you were in a meeting late in the day and felt you were able to give it your full attention, presence, and focus over the full course of the meeting? If you can recall such a time, does this happen frequently?

The answer is likely no.

How about in remote settings?

Still no.

You see, I believe we begin each day from a thriving state: our cups are full and we are like a fresh canvas ready to be painted. Our decision fatigue is the lowest it will be for the entire day. Our brains are most rested and even our blood pressure is low. From this state, it's really up to you how long you carry that thriving state with you throughout your days.

Think about how sharp you feel in the morning after a good sleep. You feel focused, energized, and ready for the day. It's as though an invisible suit of armour just parachuted down from space and covered you from head to toe. Your feet hit the floor and, if you have solid morning routines in place, you can begin to action out your morning activities.

Then, suddenly, life happens.

Meetings pop up.

Email notifications start going off.

The kids need to get ready for school.

The phone starts pushing more notifications.

The world requires your attention.

You get in the car, commute to school to drop the kids off, grab a coffee, and head either to the office or back home to start your workday. By the time you dawn the office door, are you still in a thriving state? Maybe. If you're lucky, have been able to avoid traffic, remain on time, and are really well-rested, you just may be!

However, for the vast majority, your thriving suit of armour has already been partially shed and it's only about 9:15 am.

Then, you spend the rest of the workday slowly shedding what armour is left, eventually just looking at the clock hoping it will move faster until the day is finally done.

Sound familiar? Why do you think this is?

Is it that you don't care about your work?

Absolutely not.

We shed our armour because our energy has been spent throughout the day on various tasks and responsibilities, leaving us in a naked, frail state. As the day rolls along, our ability to thrive dwindles down to nothing, and with it goes our focus, presence, willpower, and attention.

This is not our fault. Why?

Because of two main reasons:

1. Because we were never taught in school how to manage our energy. We learn a bit about how to manage money in math and we learn a bit about how to manage time through meeting our assignment and exam deadlines. However, I doubt anyone ever said to you, *"Hey, have you been monitoring and managing your energy lately?"*
2. Because society doesn't value energy, it values performance and productivity. In the corporate and government worlds, we are forced to stretch employees' capacity, often demanding more performance from them without replenishing their energy in return. In some situations, this becomes unbalanced, toxic, and unhealthy. I saw this first-hand with my father but, luckily, he was in a position of privilege and could see the writing on the wall, allowing him to decide to retire early. To this day he still thanks me from time to time for helping nudge him towards that early retirement decision.

So there you have it. We are doing more with less and expected to deliver in school and in our professional lives from a less-than-thriving state. I have seen how this story ends and it isn't good for anyone involved. Businesses think they are winning by stretching the dollar but what they are actually doing is losing in the long run. They lose in the time it takes to onboard a new employee down the road when you leave due to burnout.

You are losing in this scenario as well because society screams, *"You can achieve your dreams and goals!"* but fails to mention that by the time you can even get around to your dreams and goals, you are already energy deprived. It's like starting a race two laps down yet still hoping to somehow pull off a win.

The truth is, you need to treat our energy like it's entering a battlefield each day. You need to suit up. You need to be prepared. You need to preserve your supplies. You need to be vigilant and expect the unexpected. You need to survive the battle in one piece.

Before entering any battle, you must engage in strategic preparation. If you don't properly prepare for conditions, situations, and various ultimatums, you will likely fail. To avoid the daily failure of losing your thriving state, including your precious energy along the way, I created an energy auditing system that will allow you to pivot towards your wellbeing and away from mere survival within your remote working environment.

This energy audit stems from nearly a decade of lived experience with energy management in semi-remote or fully remote environments. Having spoken, researched, and written on this topic over the past number of years, here is the remote energy audit that I use quarterly to ensure that my energy is being spent appropriately:

Energy Audit Questions

1. When do I feel the most tired in my day and why?
2. When do I feel the most energized in my day and why?
3. What 1-2 things take the most energy from me most days?
4. Can these 1-2 things be removed, mitigated, or approached differently? If so, how would that look?
5. What 1-2 things breathe energy into my life most days?
6. Is there something else I can bring into my days that will increase my energy?

Now that you better understand, and are more consciously aware of, how your energy is actually being spent (*using the energy audit questions*), it is absolutely vital that we talk about the *five-step energy amplifier blueprint*™ that you will need to fill out to ensure you can do these three things daily:

1. **Move from *awareness* to *action***
2. **Remain in a *thriving* state well beyond 9:00 am**
3. **Sustain your *energy*, *focus*, and *attention* throughout your days, weeks, and months**

Using your journal, here is the *five-step energy amplifier blueprint*™ to shift your days from surviving to thriving.

Step 1: **Evening Routine**	Look at the day ahead. Ask yourself these introspective questions and record them in your journal: 1. Do I feel good about my morning routine tomorrow? 2. What really needs my attention the most at work tomorrow? 3. What needs my attention the least? 4. How much is this day going to require of me? Is it potentially beyond what I can manage? If so, can I move things off my list for tomorrow that are less urgent? 5. Where are there opportunities within my day to recharge? What can I do within this window to recharge? 6. How do I want to spend my energy when I am finished work for the day?

Step 1: **Evening Routine**	Here are the five <u>evening actions</u> designed to set you up for peak energy in the morning: 1. Drink at least 150 ml of water before bed 2. Minimal use of technology at least one hour before bed 3. Set out your activewear for your morning movement (*if this is part of your morning routine*) 4. Keep the bedroom distraction-free and at a slightly cooler temperature than the rest of your home 5. Automate any other tasks so that they don't need to be done in the morning such as prepping the coffee machine, or filling up your water bottle
Step 2: **Pre-Day Routine**	Questions: 1. From 0-5, how am I feeling this morning? (*5 being on top of the world*) 2. What am I grateful for today? 3. What am I most excited about today? 4. What needs my extreme focus today? 5. What is my word for the day? <u>Pre-Day Actions:</u> 1. Complete 30-60 minutes of moderate to vigorous physical activity within the first 100 minutes of waking 2. Drink at least 100 ml of cold water as soon as you wake 3. Run through your day and ponder what you are most grateful for/excited about 4. Write in your journal 5. Avoid email for at least the first 30 minutes of your morning 6. Avoid social media 'doom scrolling' for at least the first 30 minutes of your morning

Step 3: 10:00 am Mid-Morning Routine

Questions:
1. How is my focus right now?
2. How can I remain focused this morning?
3. How's my posture? My breathing?

Mid-Morning Actions:
1. Take a standing or walking break away from your desk, work environment, or screen
2. Roll your shoulders back and open up your chest
3. Take a few deep breaths
4. Drink at least 100 ml of water
5. Enjoy a healthy snack
6. Repeat, "*I am strong, I am focused, I am thriving*" a couple of times either internally or out loud

Healthy, Plant-Based Lunch

Step 4: 2:00 pm Midday Routine

Questions:
1. How is my energy, focus, and attention now compared to where it was earlier today? This morning?
2. What can I continue to do to preserve my remaining focus, energy, and attention this afternoon?
3. What do I need to change, correct, or mitigate within the rest of my day to ensure I have energy and focus left for later in the day?

Midday Actions:
1. Take a walking or standing break from your desk, work environment, or screen
2. Do a small deep breathing exercise
3. Get outside for at least 10 minutes
4. Set a micro goal regarding how you want to round out your day and outline what can be moved to the next day to realize that goal
5. Dedicate the next hour to one or two specific tasks, projects, or activities to avoid trying to accomplish too much given the time remaining in your afternoon

Step 5: Psychological Send-Off Routine	Evening Actions: 1. When the workday is done, make sure it is done - create a psychological trigger to signal when the work is done such as closing the laptop or turning off a specific light. 2. Spend the remainder of your day dedicating your focus, energy, and attention to your hobby, family, or passion project 3. Eat a healthy meal 4. Consciously work to avoid distractions and remain present in your home 5. Prepare to repeat steps 1 to 5 tomorrow

You will notice that the energy audit is front-loaded within the day. This is due to the nature of your flow of energy throughout our days. It is important to bulk the auditing process while our cups are full and your energy is still high, rather than when your cup is empty late in the day.

You will also see that "Step 1" of the *energy amplifier blueprint*™ actually occurs before the day begins. Think about this like preparing for a trip or a vacation. If you wait until the morning of your vacation to pack and plan, it usually ends up a mess and not matching what you had envisioned as a relaxing start to your time away. However, when you pack and plan the evening before, you feel much more confident starting the trip the next morning and are more likely to feel confident and relaxed going into your vacation. This *energy amplifier blueprint*™ is no different.

For the next 21 days, if you really want to go from surviving to thriving in your remote working environment, practicing the routines you build from both the quarterly audit and

the energy amplifier blueprint*™ *daily is paramount. Not only will you see the results of this audit impact your life in monumental ways, your energy will completely shift.

How you think about your energy will shift.

Who you spend your energy on may shift.

You will also begin to feel better and more in control of your days.

These are the shifts that will move you in the direction you want to go. These shifts will afford you more energy, allowing you to hyperfocus during your workday and be more present and attentive to the dreams and goals that you want to achieve within your work and personal life.

Up next I want to explore the notion that adding value is enough. Regardless of performance targets and goals, the simple act of adding value daily will set you up for success in your remote working career. Let me show you why.

Chapter 3

ADDING VALUE IS ENOUGH

*"When something is important enough,
you do it even if the odds are not in your favor."*

-Elon Musk

You have probably learned first-hand that working in remote working environments is not easy. In fact, in most cases, it is just as hard, if not harder than working in traditional office environments. Sure, certain elements of your job may have changed for the better, like working in your slippers, but good work is still good work, and that requires time, energy, passion, purpose, and a mountain of focus.

So where does performance fit into this idea of thriving remotely? How do we know if we are still performing at a high level in our remote working environment?

We know from the audit and blueprint that we are now managing our energy, focus, and attention better than ever, but that doesn't necessarily equate to high performance.

Just like everything we do, it is important to have some way of measuring the value we bring each day. However, I would caution that it is equally as important not to lose sight of the ***pure significance of adding value***, regardless of what you measure in terms of performance or productivity. Adding value digs deeper. It is attached to feelings of purpose and our belief system. So, although it is important to measure, we can't lose sight of the fact that it is a metric that goes much deeper than external measurements of performance or productivity: it is about your beliefs, purpose, and worth.

In spite of the work you do, or where you do it, the goal should always be to add value to the world through your vocation. But what does this mean and how does this look in your new way of working?

For starters, we should define value. In business, if we have a "value-add," it means that the product is ultra attractive to the consumer. The same idea can be applied to a service as well.

If value-add means a product is more likely to sell, I would argue that adding value daily makes you, and the services you offer, more attractive to who you are "selling" to as well. In essence, adding value daily should make you more attractive to your team and make the products and services you create even more attractive to the client or consumer. This is why adding value in itself is enough.

If you can find ways to add value to your work every day in remote settings, that alone is both a performance and engagement measure. Performance-wise, this means you are dedicated enough to making the product or service extra attractive and special for the user. From an engagement standpoint, this means you are actively engaged in the work that needs to get done and not just a bystander riding the coattails of your own reputation or that of your high performing peers.

At the end of the day, the challenge really becomes how to consistently add value each day, month, and year while working in a remote setting, regardless of any other indicators you may or may not be measuring (*e.g., performance*).

There is no marching band standing outside your home, ready to play a song of celebration loud enough for the entire block to hear if you nail that next email or secure that next client. Gary Vaynerchuk isn't going to call you up and be like, *"Yo, well done! You crushed it today at work."*[6]

So, how do you continue to add value each and every day when you are wearing pajamas and your environment consists of the steeping teapot, children playing, and/or a barking dog under your feet?

Here's how:

CREATE AN ACCOMPLISHMENTS SPREADSHEET

If you've read any of my work on *Medium*, you will know that I have been a huge advocate for accomplishment spreadsheets since the beginning of my career. Creating an accomplishment spreadsheet is something that I borrowed from author John C. Maxwell five years ago and I continue to use it to this day. My accomplishment spreadsheet is internal, meaning I am the only one who sees it. I use the basic Numbers iOS app on my iPad where I do two things each month. First, I look back and remind myself of the accomplishments I achieved in the previous month. Second, I record those accomplishments in chart form, whether big or small. Documenting all of these in one place not only reminds me of all that I've accomplished in the last month but also serves as a growth tool. I always enjoy skipping back a few years to see what I recorded as an accomplishment at that point in my life. I sometimes laugh and think to myself, *I can't believe I thought this was a huge accomplishment*, which, to me, indicates that I have grown since those milestones.

Creating a private accomplishment spreadsheet is the single greatest weapon you can arm yourself with when working in a remote environment. This spreadsheet can serve multiple purposes. It can serve as a way to pump your tires when the day or week just hasn't felt great. It can serve as a tool to continue to build your confidence in the remote working environment, and it can also serve as a career success runway when your annual evaluation comes around or if you need the extra confidence to ask for that raise you know you already deserve.

For you, I recommend starting a basic chart that is simple and easy for you to track. Don't overcomplicate things. The goal here is simply to record any and all accomplishments you want to track. No one but you ever needs to see it, so include everything that *you* want to include!

It is important to remember that an accomplishment spreadsheet should remain private at all times. Treat it like it's the key to your success vault. Only you can judge what constitutes success in your work, regardless of the outcome. For example, I have a spreadsheet that is years long. Each quarter, I update it with either process victories or performance victories. Process victories are things like being better at managing emails or organizing monthly expenses for my business. Performance victories are directly attributed to an outcome such as successfully delivering five speaking engagements last month. Sometimes process and performance victories converge. When they do, it is essential to break them apart into their simplest forms so that they can be tracked more easily and not lumped together. Both small and large victories count!

Here is another great example of a performance and process victory. Back in 2017, I finally started making money as an author on *Medium*, and what did I do? I recorded this milestone in the accomplishment spreadsheet. What the spreadsheet won't tell you is that I only made 20 cents per article at the time. To me, the number didn't matter; it was the fact that I was finally getting paid for bringing great thoughts to the world. This simple reflection pushed me to write even more. My writing processes improved as the performance victory flowed in, which resulted in writing 100 more articles and earning 100s of more dollars.

Decide your accomplishments.

Record your accomplishments quarterly.

Thrive.

Repeat.

BREATHE LIFE INTO YOUR JOURNAL, DAILY

If you aren't journaling and work in a remote environment, it is time to put down this book and grab yourself a journal. If you already journal, it is time to breathe even more life into it. Why? Because if you look at remote work as a way of living, journaling is the best quality of air to fill your lungs and keep you alive.

Journaling about your deepest thoughts and feelings, greatest highlights in life, and moments of gratitude worth noting are some of the best ways to bolster your wellbeing in a remote setting. Journaling keeps you conscious in a world that has become increasingly digital, expeditious, and attention-based. The simple act of writing a few words in your journal as you begin each day can help keep you grounded, organized, focused, and on point when it comes to your work tasks and various day-to-day responsibilities. ***Think of journaling as a private reflection moment that no email, meeting, obligation, or deadline can take away.*** I guess you could really think about it as a sacred ceremony of sorts. May I go so far as to say it is like going on a date with your destiny each day?

PLAN A QUARTERLY ASSESSMENT AND REFLECTION PERIOD

Along with your accomplishment spreadsheet, doing a quarterly assessment is vital if you want to thrive in remote working environments. It is an incredible way to measure your value-add to your craft. This is a strategy I recently learned from a business mentor that really stood out to me as essential. It has been monumental in staving off imposter syndrome (*more on that in the next chapter*).

I typically set three to four goals for the quarter ahead, including the indicators, results, and mechanisms I will use to reach those goals. At the end of that quarter, I pull out the sheet and assess myself on how well I did based on the plan I created. This assessment illustrates both my successes and my shortcomings, while also providing me great feedback on why I hit certain marks and where I may have fallen short with others. ***Success*** *leaves clues and this strategy allows you to find them and follow them.*

Four times a year, I set up an assessment and reflection period, which is an uninterrupted morning (*minimum of 3 hours*) where I gather my calendar, journals, and notes, throw them into a blender and look at what comes out.

My journal (*the roadmap*) often contains notes that indicate where I may have gotten complacent in the previous quarter and where I can improve in the next. When I find these gems, it's like finding change while walking along the side of the road. It makes my day and leaves me with more than what I had just a few moments ago.

My notes (*which are usually in email and paper folders*) may also contain important breadcrumbs that can be really helpful when setting goals for my next quarter. Though sometimes they contain nothing, and that is ok too.

I also look at my calendar (*which doubles as my roadmap of time spent on various projects, meetings, hobbies, etc.*) and think about where I felt good, where I may have felt overwhelmed, and what I can look ahead to in the next quarter. I typically assess my calendar in more detail, depending on the goals that I have set, the project phases I am in, and any upcoming obligations in my personal life.

For you, **I highly recommend starting a quarterly goal tracking sheet.** If you are interested in using my template, email me at faheyconsulting@gmail.com and I will send you a digital copy to help you get started.

SEEK OUT MOMENTS EACH DAY WHERE YOU FEEL YOU CAN ADD VALUE

Teachers use the term "teachable moments" to describe specific moments in time or moments that present a lesson within a lesson. When these occurred as I was teaching, I remember waiting in anticipation for Miyagi to jump out or suddenly appear in the back corner of the classroom.

In the remote working stratosphere, these moments can happen in a similar spirit. *In adding value daily, consciously look for small moments where you can add value throughout each day.* To do so, focus less on the work itself and more on the margins of the work being completed. For example, is there a unique moment during a meeting where you can add a bit more value to an idea or discussion item? Is there a way you can frame a sentence in an email that can add a bit more value to the conversation? Is there a weight you can lift off the shoulders of a colleague today to add more value to your role within your team? Does someone need extra time in your meeting just to talk or to share what's on their mind? Can you add value to someone's day by calling just to say hello?

Fulfilling any one of these questions can help you directly add small moments of value to your work in remote settings. I like to think of it as being more like Stephen Covey if Stephen was working remotely. *Seek first to understand and then take that understanding a step further by adding a flair of more value. Adding value is never a bad thing and can lead to a long, successful remote working career.*

PLAN TO ADD VALUE

Jay-Z once said, "*I believe you can speak things into existence.*" This has never been more true when it comes to adding value each day. **You can manifest value.**

When you wake, tell yourself that you will add value today. Repeat it. Then do the same while you are in the shower, doing your hair, or going through other parts of your morning routine. This is mission-critical. **Not only is this affirmation and encouragement going to help set you up for a great day, it is also telling your subconscious that you will add value, no matter what the day presents to you.**

Don't believe me? Well, if all you want to drive is a TESLA, the next time you are driving somewhere, you will likely notice more TESLA cars on the road. That doesn't necessarily mean there are more of them on the road than yesterday, it just means that subconsciously your mind is already looking for them. It wants them. The same is true with regards to looking to add value each day. When you tell yourself you will add it, your brain will start looking for ways it can be added.

As your day progresses, you will begin to see areas in the margins of your workday where you can add value. You will know these moments when you see them - just don't forget to act on them! **Don't let the sun set on the day without adding that value.** You can even set a private calendar block with that specific item you can add value to so that you don't forget to manifest it into existence.

SET A CALENDAR PROMPT
(*DID I ADD VALUE TODAY?*)

At a time where "doing more with less" is the standard operating procedure, it is quite easy to find yourself wondering, *What am I really doing with my life?* Especially at the end of a long day in a remote working environment.

To avoid this existential crisis, brought on by losing sight of the value being added, set a calendar prompt or place a memo on your fridge or pillow. This can help support you and your ability to add value daily by simply nudging you to think about all the value you added during each workday. This is not about how many emails you answered, or how productive your meetings were, **it is about how much energy, engagement, passion, and value you added to your craft for that particular day.**

Reflecting on this in your journal is a great way to remain in a thriving state while working in remote environments for the long haul (*more on the long haul later*). Plus, it will allow you to step away from the computer at the end of the day and enjoy that well-earned treat or post-work beverage of choice.

At the end of the day, you are enough, and adding value is always enough. Just because you may be more hidden in a remote setting, this does not mean you provide any less value or bring any less passion or deep sense of purpose to your craft.

In the event that you are still questioning your value at this point, it is time to address the reality that you are likely dealing with some form of imposter syndrome. It's time to thrive, not to doubt. In the next chapter, we are going to send that little gremlin packing.

Chapter 4

OVERCOMING IMPOSTER SYNDROME

"To attain 'success' without attaining positive self-esteem is to be condemned to feeling like an imposter anxiously awaiting exposure."
-Nathaniel Branden

There is nothing more crushing than showing up to your job each day, adding value, and a bucket of passion, only to be given negative feedback or criticism of your work.

Pouring your heart, soul, and precious currency of time into your work, whether at home or the office, is something to take a tremendous amount of pride in. ***It is essential that you love what you do as a craft as that drives you forward and gives you a deep sense of purpose.*** However, no matter how hard you work, how much value you bring to your work, or how much time you spend doing the absolute best work possible, somewhere, at some point, someone is going to complain about what you've done. If you work in any industry that deals with customer service, client retention, or services and sales, you know exactly what I'm talking about.

As you take a moment to reflect on a specific situation or moment in time where you recall this criticism hitting you in the teeth, you are not alone.

Here is a children's story version of the various characters that exist in the remote work setting that you will need to be consciously aware of:

1. The Snake - These folks are tricky to identify, as they are outwardly nice, methodical, and on point; however, **you have to be extra cautious with them because you can't be sure if they are poisonous or not.** Snakes exist everywhere and in various forms. They can be identified in virtual meetings by the way they speak and act, or they can show up via back-end channels and attempt to bite you in the rear end. The best way to deal with snakes is to be proactive and protect yourself. Always double-check your work and be sure you can back up everything you have signed your John Hancock just in case one tries to bite.

2. The Shark - Unlike snakes, **sharks are more obvious and territorial.** They behave audaciously and, seemingly, have more of an aggressive presence than the rest of us. Within minutes of encountering them, you will be able to identify them. They are often the loudest in the room (*or online*) and will be direct and bold. The only way to deal with the shark is to treat them like a shark. Being bold and refusing to back down from a shark will cause them to respectfully retreat or face even more tension with you, your team, or your cause.

3. The Spider - *The spider is naturally calm but always ready to strike at a moment's notice, especially once its web is spun.* You will notice them in the room as they seem obtuse and may make the hair on the back of your neck stand up every now and again. When they strike, it is usually abrupt so as to catch you by surprise. Once you are tangled up in the web of emotion from the strike, it is too late. The moment has passed and you are unfortunately left to deal with your own emotions after the fact.

The best way to deal with a spider is to always watch your back and pour yourself an extra cup of coffee ahead of the meeting, just in case they strike. You will want to be sharp and direct in a rebuttal to avoid getting caught in the web. For a spider, being ready is key.

These bone-chilling creatures all exist in the workforce. In their presence, you can easily be torn down - any time, anywhere. Even the best companies in the world deal with them. **Nature is nature, regardless of the walls and desks that are put in the ecosystem.**

This teardown, among other factors like burnout and/or low-level confidence, can steer us toward what is commonly known as "Imposter Syndrome."

Imposter syndrome is defined in *Psychology Today* as, *"a psychological term referring to a pattern of behavior where people doubt their accomplishments and have a persistent, often internalized fear of being exposed as a fraud."*[7]

While this is not an actual medical disorder in most circles, it is still a lethal pattern of behavior brought on by various circumstances in life that many struggle with. In remote working environments, this 'syndrome' may already be amplified, even without the presence of all the critters mentioned above. All it takes is one strike from one critter or a blow in your personal life for the poison of imposter syndrome to set in.

Signs of imposter syndrome look different for everyone depending on the various work contexts you find yourself in. However, some overarching patterns can be identified that, if experienced, will help reveal to you if this is something you are struggling with.

Some notable signs that you are struggling with imposter syndrome may be:

- Feeling an internal fear of public failure
- Feeling the need to say "yes" to everything that is asked of you
- Feeling that you need to work longer hours to achieve more in your work
- Feeling anxious when being asked to speak to someone with a "bigger" title and more experience than you
- Feeling that you are not enough after even one unproductive day at work
- Feeling that others are achieving more and are more competent at your job than you with no real evidence
- Feeling that you are dispensable, even in permanent positions, with no real evidence to justify that you are underperforming
- Feeling that no matter how hard you work, you are never enough
- Waking up in the evening and thinking about what you need to do at work

If any combination of the above feelings or symptoms have polluted your days, weeks, or even months, you are not alone! Many professionals around the world suffer from various degrees of this syndrome.

Working remotely does not automatically give us a diploma or certify us as qualified to navigate these feelings either. Here is an excellent visual which visually articulates the cycle of imposter syndrome.

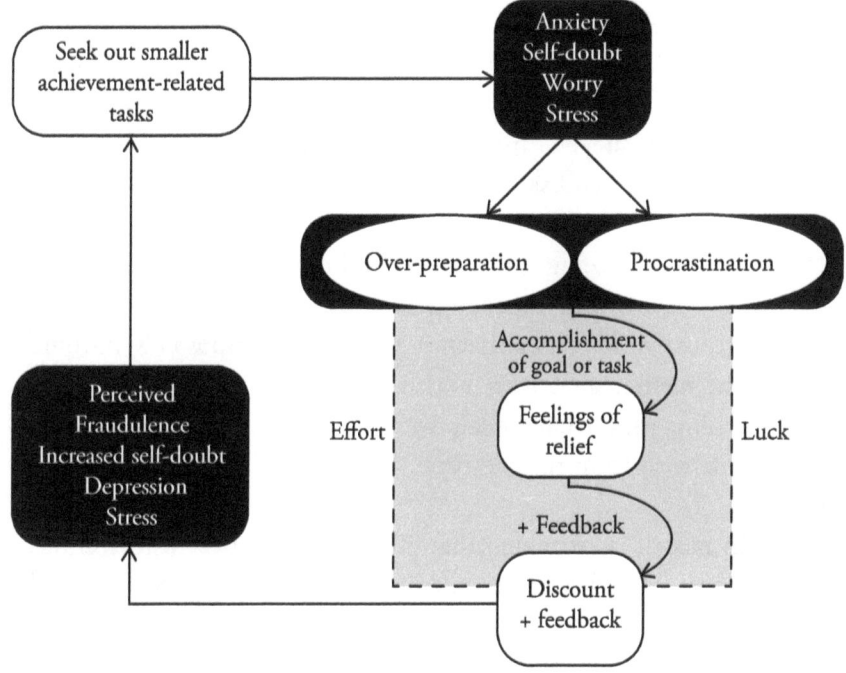

Adapted from Clance's (1985) model of the Imposter Cycle (as cited in Craig, 2018).

Craig, L. (2018, September). *Are you suffering from imposter syndrome? Ways to identify and deal with feelings of self-doubt in grad school.* American Psychological Association.

From the visual, you can infer that anxiety, self-doubt, worry, stress, and fear of failure all feed into the cycle of imposter syndrome. As the cycle goes, you resort to either procrastination or over-preparation for a given task. After it is complete, you will feel a deep sense of relief but it is usually short-lived. If you are lucky enough to still be getting positive feedback on your work, that can easily be discounted, which, over time, leads to the manifestation of more chronic components of the syndrome, allowing for long-term self-doubt, depression, stress, and anxiety to settle into your soul. As a result, you only seek out tasks that you can more easily accomplish to avoid these feelings altogether. Simply put, you revert to survival mode rather than continuing to step into your true talent and skills.

As you are seeing, the presence of imposter syndrome in your system poisons your capacity for remote thrivability. It is impossible to thrive if you experience any level of imposter syndrome in your mental diet. I know this because imposter syndrome is something that I have dealt with in the past and continue to struggle with from time to time.

In fact, it is estimated that 70% of people deal with feelings of imposter syndrome at least once in their lives.[8] Never mind adding in a layer of complexity with the emotions inherent to working in a remote setting, mostly in isolation. Unfortunately, imposter syndrome does not magically disappear either.

Remote work environments can make us even more susceptible to the cycle of imposter syndrome. This is due to many factors, some of which are:

1. An inability to read physical body language easily
2. An inability to properly understand communication tones at all times
3. An inability to engage in "water cooler conversations" before and after meetings to validate how you may be feeling
4. An inability to accurately read the room before speaking

Couple this with the screaming kids in the background and the cat needing to be fed and you can easily fall down the rabbit hole of imposter syndrome. Attempting to balance our responsibilities in the home with the responsibilities of our crafts can cause us to feel like we are always falling short. This can become a vicious cycle and often leave us turning to that bottle of wine or the nostalgia of classic Disney movies to drown out these feelings because it takes too much of what little energy we have left in our days to deal with them.

While the wine may work temporarily, it won't work long term. **Relief from the feelings of imposter syndrome is different from restoration from it all together.** If we are going to thrive in remote environments, it is time to deal with imposter syndrome head-on. Here is a list of strategies to help you avoid and eliminate this syndrome from your life:

SEEK OUT A MENTOR

Seeking out a mentor is one of the most important things you can do in your life when you are working remotely. **Having an emotionally safe space to retreat to is just as important as having an emotionally safe person to talk things over with.** Ever since I started my remote working journey almost a decade ago, having 1-2 mentors to lean on has been absolutely essential for me. I treat my conversations with them as a healthcare appointment. Some mentors I connect with quarterly, others monthly, and others I even connect with weekly. Having conversations with a mentor is like getting the flu shot for imposter syndrome. You may still be at some level of risk to get bouts of it throughout your year, but your chances are significantly lower now that you have an effective vaccination via your frequent dosage of mentorship.

To seek out a mentor, you must first look to those who are closest to you. Of that group, whom do you admire most? Who do you want to emulate in some way? Once you know the answer to these questions, a shortlist of mentors will unveil itself to you.

From there, initiate and remain intentional with the mentor you choose to bring into your life more closely. Be authentic, practice active listening, and be open as well as flexible. As Disney's The Mandalorian would say, *"This is the way."*

GET CLEAR AND SIMPLE WITH EACH TASK

KISS imposter syndrome goodbye by keeping things clear and simply simplistic.

For one reason or another, our world seems to want to find ways to overcomplicate things. Inefficiencies and superfluous red tape are everywhere. Our lives are shaped by structures and policies that dictate our every move, and we don't even realize it. These complexities are everywhere, including the language we use to describe our work. For example, think about the term "structural engineer." What do they do? Well, I'd imagine they build structures like bridges. So, why don't their business cards simply say, *"Hi, I'm Ryan and I build bridges."*

A few years ago, I was hired to help run an event. When I was putting together the program and reading all of the session descriptions, I noticed that they were filled with jargon, as were many of the featured biographies. So, for my biography I wrote "Human Being" as my title under my name. I wanted people to understand that I am a human being first and foremost. At the end of the day, isn't that what matters most?

Simple.

Clear.

Concise.

In our complex world, the best rule you can implement in your remote environment is to keep it simply simplistic (*KISS*). If you can mitigate the level of complexity in your life, it will become exponentially better.

As a perfect example, I was once thrown into a remote project mid-stride. When I entered the first project meeting, I hardly understood any of the language being used. I thought to myself, *None of this makes sense, and I don't know why! I am the perfect person to lead this project and have been working in the sector for years... What is wrong with me???* Cue the imposter gremlin!

Turns out, absolutely nothing was wrong with me or my skills - everyone in the room just decided to use a thesaurus when talking about the project. This caused so much inefficiency and frustration for me early on in the project that it likely cost the organization a week's worth of work on time spent trying to understand the lingo.

Once I figured out that everything being said was just framed in fancier language than I would use, I was able to manage the project using KISS. I stopped using glorified, over-complicated language in my meetings and in my work and decided that I would keep things super clear and simple for folks.

If there are things that you come across that just seem overly complicated or unclear, try using this acronym to approach the work and how you manage it. I guarantee your life will become easier and that you will be able to get back to thriving in your remote working environment. Because with clarity comes comfort of mind.

OWN YOUR WORD

If you say you will deliver, deliver. If you say you can't deliver, own that too! If you want to avoid imposter syndrome, ***your word is everything, always.*** Giving your word that you will get something done is a social contract, and contracts require trust in order to work. Building trust and strengthening relationships based on your word will allow you to continue moving forward in your remote working environment while also helping you avoid the onset of imposter syndrome. If you speak something into being, you need to own it and take responsibility for getting it done.

TAKE OWNERSHIP

Similar to owning your word, you need to own your work and its results. In a performance-driven society, someone needs to own success. Why can't that be you? ***Taking ownership of your work and what needs to get done is essential to being successful and thriving in remote working environments.*** This could mean you lose a Saturday evening every now and again, but taking ownership and leading what you have committed or been committed to is integral. Own the good and the bad. If you make a mistake on a project, you need to own that as equally as you own the success of another. Ownership builds trust within your team and within yourself. ***Internal trust within yourself builds confidence and a high level of confidence allows no room for imposter syndrome.***

FIND SMALL WINS

If you find you are struggling with imposter syndrome, changing your performance metrics and outlook may be the key to begin thriving again in your remote working environment. When you shift your focus from catching the big fish or nailing that big contract to the small wins, it doesn't mean that you aren't successful or aren't doing a great job. It just means you've shifted your focus; that's it!

When you focus on achieving small wins, the big wins come.

Growing up, I was an average baseball player. From an early age, I knew my place on the team. I was not the home run hitter; I was the guy who would single or double you to death because once I was on base, I was a real threat to score. I stole bases, which made pitchers nervous and threw them off their game. I always focused on what is commonly called "small ball." This allowed me to contribute to the team each year and to be a decent player. I have no home run records. In fact, I've only hit two home runs in my 10-year amateur baseball career. But that doesn't matter. I focused on small wins. The stolen bases. The base hits. The bunts. The walks. Once I got onto a base, I knew I could do more damage. We won a lot of games that way. Even at the highest level in baseball, many games are won by teams who park their egos and own their roles as either small ball or home run hitting baseball players.

The same is true in your remote work. If you can focus on the small daily or weekly wins, eventually the big wins come. You will get where you need to go. You just need to work your magic in manufacturing the small wins. If you do, the big ones will eventually come. Like me, you may only hit a couple of home runs in your career but those will be worth celebrating. If you are a small ball player, own that day in and day out for long-term success. Focusing on your area of strength and tracking your small wins are critical to either climb out of the imposter rabbit hole or avoid the rabbit hole altogether.

These strategies, along with what was laid out in Chapters 2 and 3 of this book, will be invaluable in helping you mitigate or avoid imposter syndrome altogether in your remote working environment. ***Know your value, trust your value, and deliver daily.*** If you do this and deploy many of the strategies outlined in this book, you will set yourself up to thrive in your remote working environment.

In the next chapter, I will share with you what happens when you overcome imposter syndrome and begin working from your skill areas and why book smarts alone may not be enough in this new way of working.

Chapter 5

DEVELOPING YOUR EQ OVER YOUR IQ

"What really matters for success, character, happiness, and life long achievements is a definite set of emotional skills – your EQ — not just purely cognitive abilities that are measured by conventional IQ tests."
-Daniel Goleman

In remote working environments, it is imperative that you develop your emotional skills (EQ) to be able to thrive. According to the World Economic Forum, emotional intelligence was ranked number 6 on the top 10 skills needed for success in the 2020s.[9]

So what is EQ anyway?

For starters, EQ is the greatest professional discovery since the internet. Although the origin of the term is mixed, the common consensus is that Peter Salovey, a former junior professor at Yale University, now the university's President, coined the term. According to the Institute for Health and Human Potential, emotional intelligence is defined as the ability to "recognize, understand, and manage our own emotions and recognize, understand, and influence the emotions of others."[10]

In more practical terms, ***it means being aware that emotions can drive our behavior and impact others,*** and it means learning how to manage those emotions – both our own and others'. The ability to manage our emotions is especially important in situations when we are under pressure or duress. Some remote working examples include:

- Giving and receiving feedback
- Meeting tight deadlines
- Dealing with challenging relationships
- Not having enough (*or adequate*) resources
- Navigating change or change management
- Working through setbacks and failure

The ability to navigate the emotions that can bubble up from any one of these examples is an indicator of the strength of your EQ.

Now, without diving too deep into the societal need for intellectual intelligence (*measured by one's IQ*) and the professional need for emotional intelligence (*measured by one's EQ*), let's unpack how you can further enhance your EQ so that you can thrive in your remote working environment.

I once had a remote position that required me to have a firm pulse on the nation's stance within a specific space. One day my wife came out of the bedroom and saw me pacing around my remote office space in our apartment. When she asked me what I was doing, I think I said something to the effect of, *"I am just taking a moment to sense what needs to get done for the organization and our community in this next hour."*

We then had a brief chat about careers when she suddenly asked, *"I wonder if I could do your job?"*

To which I respectfully responded, *"Hunny, as brilliant as you are in your career and within your specific work, my job requires some very unique and specific skills, including understanding what the sector needs from Vancouver Island to Newfoundland, sometimes in a moment's notice. I don't know if saying that you could just jump in and do my job is accurate."* I went on to say, *"There are skills in your profession that you have acquired that I do not possess either. In no way could I do your job."*

That conversation is a perfect example of the difference between IQ and EQ. My wife has a high-level IQ and, yes, she could really do anything she set her heart to. She also has a high-level EQ, especially as it relates to the skills needed for her profession of choice. But our jobs are inherently different and the culture, skills, and competencies required to be successful in both positions are very unique. Skills from one don't necessarily transfer to the other and vice versa.

Working with people from remote environments requires unique skill sets like the awareness to know what needs to be done for one individual in a remote part of the world, as well as the ability to sense when you just need to pick up the phone and call rather than send an email. Intuition trumps intellect.

These types of awareness are incredible assets necessary to thrive in remote working environments, especially if you are working with people. No degree, certification, or designation can teach you these skills in their entirety. You must develop them independent of your intellect in order to thrive in remote working environments.

Yes, sometimes you just need to call a colleague about something that can't be said in an email. Sometimes you just need to be direct and upfront with your boss on something rather than going through all of the operational channels set up in your place of work. And sometimes you just need to say what needs to be said regardless of what your intellect is telling you. Sometimes you just need bold candor.

Every now and again in my remote office, I look up to my left and see one of my degrees hanging on the wall, beautifully displayed in an overly expensive frame. That's it, I just look at it. I can't do anything with it. I mean, I guess I could flaunt it on LinkedIn or something but who really cares? It looks more and more like an antique every day.

While I take a tremendous amount of pride in earning my degree, there is a saying that goes something like this, "*What got you here isn't going to get you there.*" And while the degree is a nice artifact to look at and reflect on, much of it represents the intelligence, dedication, and resilience that got me here - not necessarily all the skills that will get me to where I want to go. For example, my degree doesn't represent my ability to read the tone of voice on the other end of that call or email or how well I can diffuse a live disaster on Zoom.

For this, I lean almost solely on my EQ, which is a series of soft skills and competencies.

Here is a core competency framework developed by Daniel Goleman, which breaks EQ down into its four key domains.

Adapted from Key Step Media. (n.d.). *Building blocks of emotional intelligence: 12 leadership competency primers.*

As you can see in the image, the four domains and 12 competencies of emotional intelligence are about *self* and *relationships*. You are probably already noticing how each of these comes into play within your remote working life as well. For example, ***if you are self-aware within your work, you are likely able to continue to meet deadlines, manage your energy, and achieve success within your work each day.*** You know what needs to be done and are aware of your strengths, limitations, and what you need to focus on at a given moment in time.

Similarly, you will have a strong ability to manage relationships as you develop your EQ. This goes back to the story I told earlier around understanding the one specific need of one specific individual within one specific part of the world. ***Brokering strong relationships is absolutely essential to thriving in remote working environments when you find yourself dealing with people.*** Within your team, this involves focusing your attention, active listening, and being able to manage conflict as it arises, to name a few important skills.

Social awareness is one domain that I find very interesting for remote workers. Here's why:

During the first winter of the COVID-19 pandemic, an opportunity arose for me to continue to work remotely but in a more rural part of Canada. Operationally, nothing was different. However, logistically, everything would need to be looked at and assessed from an organizational standpoint before a decision was made to relocate my remote office. I needed to schedule test virtual meetings, seek proactive advice from our IT department, and formulate some backup plans if my remote connection wasn't as good as it needed to be in this alternate setting. Simply put, I knew that the decision to move to another remote location not only needed to work for me, it needed to work for the organization as well. There needed to be little to no hiccups with the transition so that the efficiency and connectivity between myself and my team were not compromised.

This is a great example of being aware of what the organization needs from a logistical and connectivity lens in a remote working environment. This is social awareness from an organizational viewpoint.

At the end of the day, ***developing your EQ is really about developing competencies that enhance your human potential while building a system around those competencies that allows you, your team, and your organization to thrive.***

This development helps you thrive remotely. Applying what you learned in the first four chapters of this book, along with the strategies derived from Daniel Goleman's visual representation, will continue to set you up to thrive within your remote working environment. If you find the topic of EQ to be interesting, I would encourage you to check out more of Daniel Goleman's work, some of which I list in my book recommendations at the end of this book.

I would also encourage you to nudge your organization to further explore the EQ competency primers created by Daniel and his team so that your entire organization can dive deeper into this essential condition for success and thrivability together.

In the next chapter, we will circle back to routines and how they can be tweaked with the new knowledge you've gained. Specifically, we will narrow in on sleep and physical activity routines. As Matthew McConaughey states in his book, *Greenlights*, create structure so you can have freedom.[11] Without respecting this relationship, we cannot thrive.

Chapter 6

ROUTINE IS EVERYTHING

"Routine is not one thing. Routine is everything."

In Chapter 2, you read a bit about how routines are essential to creating thriving conditions within your remote working environment. Although this cannot be stated enough, developing hourly, daily, weekly, and monthly routines are paramount for success, fulfillment, and wellbeing in remote working environments. In this chapter, I want to focus on two specific routine areas:

1. Physical Activity Routines
2. Sleep Routines

Back in winter of 2019, the COVID-19 pandemic changed the fabric of the world. In fact, many of you reading this probably experienced contactless delivery for the first time and saw your work shift immediately to being fully remote.

I can recall the first month of the pandemic where everyone was scrambling. Zoom bombs were going off everywhere and people were still trying to figure out what they should wear at their home office for a meeting, among other things.

Within the chaos and confusion of such a tectonic shift in the way many organizations had been operating, I personally had to do some soul searching to become even better at remote work. At this point, I had been involved in temporary or part-time remote work for some time but I had to reach a new level of comfort with this new way of living. Balancing 50-60 hours of remote work was feeling much different than balancing 10-15 hours pre-pandemic.

This is why I decided to start a new morning routine, implementing a "soft start" whereby I commit to starting work sometime between 8:00 am and 9:00 am each day. This allowed me to either start and finish my workday a bit earlier or a bit later, depending on the demands of the day. It also gave me some buffer time in the morning to take care of myself, my wife, and our home before I officially began my workday.

Ultimately, this time buffing routine allowed me to better control the demands of my environment without those demands controlling me. *This, in turn, enabled me to curb any stress, anxiety, or feelings of being on edge before starting my workday, setting me up for greater chances of success.* Many remote workers can agree that flexibility is a huge must when working remotely. Building a time buffer routine within your workday is a great way to manage tasks and responsibilities in the grey spaces between work and home life.

I also decided to take a routines-based approach to thrive even more in my remote working environment. Within the rules and public health guidelines at the time, I moved my traditional morning workouts fully outside. My strength training regime landed me on an abandoned playground or near a cluster of tires that were once used for group boot camps. Even in the depths of winter, my runs migrated to the curious exploration of new routes closeby which actually allowed me to see my local community from new angles. I also drastically changed my mindset from training for what would have been a great year of performance racing to moving every day for my general health and wellbeing alone.

Cementing this morning routine allowed me to stay grounded, focused, and ready for "the office" after getting my heart pumping in the northern morning air each morning.

In his book *The Power of Habit*, Charles Duhigg talks about keystone habits, which, when activated, catalyze the activation of other important habits. Making daily physical activity a routine *(aka. a keystone habit)* is one way to facilitate the falling into place of other habits throughout the remainder of your day. For example, if you are vigorously active for at least 30 minutes per day, your body releases chemicals that make you feel better. It also suppresses leptin, which is the hormone that regulates your appetite. This hormone suppression means you will feel less hungry, which can directly result in the habit of eating less as you will experience fewer cravings for processed foods throughout the day. This, in turn, helps you manage your energy better and makes you feel good about what you are eating and when. Yes, this by-product is a result of the keystone habit of engaging in at least 30 minutes of moderate to vigorous physical activity before your day starts. One action can change your daily trajectory.

Additionally, one of the most underrated parts of our lives that we can almost constantly improve is the quality of our sleep - the keyword being "quality." In 2020, Canada released its new integrated movement guidelines which stated that Canadian adults should be getting between 7-9 hours of quality sleep with consistent waking and going to bed times.[12] Really what the guidelines, and its advocates, promote is a consistent, high-quality sleep routine! In Chapter 2, I shared some ideas around evening routines that can help facilitate the conditions for a night of quality sleep. This part of our lives should always be taken seriously if we want to thrive in our remote working environment.

Being active each day, along with the act of getting quality sleep, are critical if you want to consistently thrive in your remote working environment. By instituting the routines from Chapter 2 along with these two keystone habits - daily movement and a good night's sleep - you are creating a cocktail of success that will just get sweeter over time.

In your own remote setting, take a moment to reflect on how you can tweak your physical activity and sleep routines to help you better create thriving conditions in your remote work setting.

Here are some key questions to consider:

1. Should I rise an hour earlier?
2. How can I work my morning routine around my family's schedule?
3. Should I prepare for my workout before the next day even starts?
4. Should I schedule a buffer of 30 minutes at the start of each day to complete any necessary tasks around the house?
5. How can I adjust my physical activity routine if there is bad weather?
6. How can I use my phone to help me get better sleep?

Doing this short inquiry by answering these six questions will help you identify where you can make further tweaks in your physical activity and sleep routines, reduce the likelihood of remote burnout, and enhance your thriving conditions. Remember, the secret to thriving in a remote working environment is to develop solid, holistic routines in all areas of our lives. ***Routine is not one thing, it is everything.***

Using the following pages, or your own journal, I want to encourage you to write down some thoughts around how you can tweak your sleep and physical activity routines to continue to set yourself up to thrive daily. What needs to change? What can you start, stop, and continue doing to better pave the way for keystone habits to take hold?

One key ingredient to thriving remotely is recognizing that distractions are still inevitable, regardless of where you do your craft. In the next chapter I am going to surface the new distractions that penetrate our focus and if unchecked, can reduce our thrivability in remote settings.

Chapter 7

SWAPPING DISTRACTIONS

"The single greatest asset we have in the 2020s is our focused attention."

Working remotely is one of the most unique aspects of being alive in the 2020s. The opportunity to work from the comforts of your own home can provide a deep sense of fulfillment.

However, there are trade-offs to this comfort, and remote work does not come without its share of distractions. Prior to my full-time job going remote, I recall many days at the office where I would get caught up in conversation, chatting about life with coworkers, and taking longer than usual lunches. I also remember often feeling distracted during meetings as email notifications, memos, and messages came in like wildfire. Needless to say, distractions in the traditional office setting were plentiful.

According to a University of California Irvine study, it takes an average of 23 minutes and 15 seconds to get back to the task after you are interrupted.[13] Yes, interruptions matter! While things like Zoom may have replaced the water cooler talk and extended lunches, you will need to manage and/or mitigate new sources of distraction and inefficiency in remote work settings to thrive remotely.

In adjusting to this new way of working, it is imperative that we guard ourselves against simply swapping distractions. What do I mean by this? Well, below is a list of some common in-office distractions (*left column*) and their remote setting relatives (*right column*). Swapping one old distraction with one new distraction is not the goal. The goal is to recognize the new distraction as a cousin to the old one and to address it head-on in your work.

In-Office Setting Distraction	Remote Setting Distraction
Coworker/client interruptions at your desk	Family/pet distractions at your desk (*e.g, the dog barking, kids screaming, etc.*)
Water cooler talk	Talking with your partner or family when you are not at your desk
Long in-person meetings	Long virtual meetings
Fire drills	Home alarms, the postal service, Amazon delivery, etc.
Overhearing office phone conversations	Overhearing conversations in your own home
Meeting interruptions	A bad internet connection

As you can see, just because we may have changed environments, it does not mean distractions are no longer abundant. I'm sure there are even more distractions not listed here that you find yourself dealing with in your own context.

The best way to start managing new distractions encountered in remote work settings is to start by simply recognizing that they exist and that they are part of the remote environment whether we like it or not. ***Life happens, and distractions are inevitable.***

After recognizing the new distractions comes awareness, management, then elimination. As a remote worker, you must already have a level of trust with your employer and you must have some level of competence and expertise to do the work you are doing. Knowing this, you will have to decide for yourself which distractions can be managed, which can be mitigated, and which can be eliminated altogether. For example, you cannot realistically tell your kids not to interrupt you for 8 hours every day. They are kids, you love them, and they have needs within those 8 hours, which, if ignored, would be neglect! Hence, distractions from kids can be managed but not eliminated. If you are to thrive in your remote work setting, forecasting time for these types of distractions - to help manage the home without it completely managing you - is a new form of mastery and could be another whole book on it's own.

For other distractions, it is essential to build strategies to help reduce their capacity to pull you from your important, focused work. This is a precondition to thriving in your remote work. At the end of the day, vocation and distraction do go hand-in-hand as life continues to move faster than ever with more distractions and an increased likelihood that you will lose focus.

Earlier in this book, I explored topics like focus, attention, and how we live in an attention-based society with our clunky, 2,000-year-old brain. So, what does this mean for longevity within your remote work? In the next chapter, I will unpack what this looks like for you and how you can remain effective over the long haul and continue to add value daily in your remote working environment.

For now, consider the ability to identify, manage, and even eliminate the distractions unique to remote work one of the most important skills for thriving in remote working environments. *If you can master the pattern of recognition, action, and mitigation/elimination, you can work virtually anywhere in the world with ease, forever.* This alone makes you more employable than others who may be just as qualified as you on paper. Exude confidence by completing high-quality work that is as free as possible from distraction and you will soon find yourself feeling even more comfortable and capable in your remote working environment.

Use this chart or your own journal to highlight the remote distractions you face and any strategies you can use to mitigate or eliminate distractions during your workday.

Remote Distraction	Mitigation/Elimination Strategies

A SINGULAR WORK SPACE

One sure way to mitigate or eliminate distractions within the remote work setting is to create one cozy, comfortable space where you can work on your craft. *I cannot emphasize enough how important it is to have one space for the majority of your remote work.* If you are going to be working on your craft 40 hours per week, 50 weeks per year, that means you are spending 2,000 hours per year working. Wouldn't you rather spend those 2,000 hours in a comfortable space?

Having one particular space in your home that psychologically triggers you to do your work, without compromising your body posture or mental health, is key for thriving remotely. If you currently find yourself working from the kitchen island some days and on the bed other days, I would recommend narrowing in on a selective vocation space that you can call home for those 2,000 hours. Your ideal space may be well lit and vibrant or it may be dim and more *hygge*.[14] It may include things like plants, an above-ground window, and space for your pet to come to visit, or it may be simplistic and minimal. Either way, once you have established this all-important *singular* workspace, I guarantee it will facilitate the work triggers you need to focus on your work by helping you manage, mitigate, and eliminate outside distractions.

While it may be impossible to fully eliminate every distraction that comes your way throughout a lengthy remote working career, recognizing distractions and building strategies to reduce or eliminate those impacting you now will assist you in better recognizing and eliminating future distractions if and/or when they arise. This will ensure that you can continue to bring your best and work from a thriving state for years to come.

Next, we will talk about maturing with remote work. Like the abrupt evolution of remote work on mass, how you do your remote work will change as systems develop and the ways you work mature. Understanding and embracing this maturity with a learning mindset will be key to success in a career filled with high-quality remote work.

Chapter 8

MATURING WITH REMOTE WORK

"Remote work is here to stay."

Let's be honest, anyone can handle remote work for 30 days. Some may even be able to survive 90 days with some support, great coffee, and a few tools. But this chapter is one that focuses on remote work extending beyond 90 days; it is about maturing with your remote work as a long hauler.

At this point in your remote work experience, you are likely either exploring remote work or currently find yourself in a situation where remote work is part of your indefinite future. If so, and you have survived the first 30, 90, or maybe even 365+ days of working remotely, consider yourself part of the 'long hauler' association. You've got the t-shirt and know what it means - and maybe what it takes - to work remotely. Kudos to you!

As I write this manuscript, it has been over a year since I became a full-time remote worker. I've watched all the seasons change through my home office window, from the budding of fresh tulips in May to the darkest mornings of mid-December. I have seen all four seasons through the lens of this new way of working. When I look back at my journal entries from a year ago I can't help but smile because I can see my growth as a long hauler.

How To Thrive In Remote Working Environments

As you read in Chapter 3, working remotely is not as easy as we once thought it was. But continuing to mature with your work while seeking out new ideas, strategies, and tools to better equip yourself for thriving in this long haul journey of remote work is paramount, if not essential, as you continue on your remote working journey.

So, in an effort to do just that - so that you can thrive into the future of remote work - it's time to talk about your ability to mature within your remote work.

When we look back just 25 short years ago, remote work was not much more than an idea. Fast forward to the 2020s and, globally, over 55% of businesses have some form of remote working option.[15]

This explosion of growth in remote work means we need to understand that just as the internet was an infant in the 90s, so too is remote work now - and what it looks like for each one of us. Think about the Zoom platform as an example. Pre-pandemic, I remember working with some clients who had no idea what Zoom even was. Plus, the functionalities of that platform were not nearly as sophisticated as they are now. Insert a global pandemic and the platform seemed to become part of the periodic table overnight. So much so that the next generation of workers will know how to use it just like they know how to use a smartphone, app-based banking, and Uber.

Sure, the disruption caused by the pandemic accelerated the development of remote working tools and platforms, like Zoom, but how we interact with them is still similar to how a toddler learns to speak: by trial and error. As I write this book, we still have systems that we can't get to talk to each other. We still have a need for YouTube tutorials teaching us how to use different remote work platforms. We also still have USB drives kicking around that we may need to use now and again, and we are still somewhat skeptical about asking a Google Home to help us with something. *The rate of innovation and development of remote working platforms and tools have outpaced our ability to manage, understand, and sometimes trust them.* In baby terms, we are still trying to say our first few words between gulps of apple sauce, and we haven't yet graduated to solid foods.

As we muddle through this relationship in our long-term remote working environments, we are going to continue needing to upskill and learn new content management systems. *Additionally, we are going to have to learn how to replicate remote environments that maximize efficiency and productivity, without taking away from our personal lives, comfortable living spaces, and the various responsibilities that come with being a working professional in the 2020s.* This will become especially true if you decide to move to a new place while still owning your craft. For example, could you be just as productive and efficient with your work if you moved to Costa Rica tomorrow?

As you continue to mature with the remote working tools that we have access to, it is vital that your attention and consciousness matures as well. *The ability to filter information, avoid duplication of work, and be able to understand the many new systems that come into play are must-have skills, especially in the context of your future work.* As you grow and gain more experience over time in remote settings, what you put our attention towards matters. *You will need to be nimble to adapt to new and changing technologies, and you will need to remain flexible as the pace of innovation continues to streamline your work.*

For example, would you be ready if your boss called you tomorrow and said, "*Our company is no longer using email. We are using this new method of communication instead.*" This is an absolute reality in a long remote working career. Pivots can happen overnight. Innovation will always outpace humanity and it will continually push us to adapt and to change to the new tools, resources, and conditions that we are presented with. Staying vigilant and not becoming complacent in your remote working environment is going to help you navigate the pace of innovation. ***Rigid flexibility is essential.***

Rigid flexibility is a phrase I coined back in my early days as a personal trainer. I would reference it with clients, stressing that while it's great to set a rigid plan, within that plan you need to remain flexible so that you can adapt to anything that comes your way. The same holds true for thriving remotely. ***Be rigid in the sense that you trust what you know to work but flexible and open to adapt to the new systems, platforms, and routines that you will need in the future.***

As we embark on longer and longer careers led by the unique ability to work remotely within a wide variety of environments, rigid flexibility with systems, tools, resources, and, yes, even other humans, will add to your employability knapsack.

Make no mistake about it: remote work is here to stay, and how you work will continue to mature over time. ***Maturity is the by-product of invention. We must respect it and embrace it for what it is.***

As someone who is excited about innovation and the prospects of a better future, especially as it relates to remote work, I am optimistic that remote work will continue to grow and expand as we continue to pour money, time, and resources into this industry. Staying ahead of the curve of innovation while always remaining open to what comes next will keep you in a thriving state, void of imposters, and confident in your day-to-day approach to your craft. You will need to continue to stay vigilant and continue to approach each day as a new opportunity to learn.

With maturity comes growth. And with growth comes the opportunity to build (*or refine*) new skills. In the next chapter, I will dive more into the specific skills that are going to be needed as remote work continues to mature. Think of it as a remote working employability skills blueprint.

Chapter 9

THE NEW SKILLS NEEDED FOR REMOTE WORK

"Focus is now the lifeblood of this economy."
- Cal Newport

It would be remiss to finish this book without talking about the new skills that are needed for thriving in remote working environments. Although this book primarily focuses on *conditions, strategies,* and *routines,* it is hard to separate skills from the conversation around thriving remotely.

Each year, LinkedIn produces a report that reveals global business insights. Of the many neat tidbits of information they share in this report, I am always most fascinated by the section detailing what skills are likely to be needed in the coming year. These projections, which are based on expertise and data, are very insightful and frequently on point.

When I look at this report annually, I am always reminded of Carol Dweck's work around a personal growth mindset, which is absolutely critical for thriving in remote working environments. (*See my book recommendations at the end of this book for more information about Carol's work around growth mindset.*)

It is necessary to adopt a personal growth mindset with regard to the new skills that are needed for remote work. Over these next few pages, I will show you the seven skills that I believe are crucial for yourself and your team to ride the wave of success and longevity together, especially when it comes to remote work. These seven skills range from conducting science experiments to the simple yet rare skill of being a good human; but if you can master them - while also implementing the other tools and strategies for thriving remotely found in this book - you will be well on your way to realizing a successful, sustainable remote working career.

#1 BEING HUMAN AND STAYING CREATIVE

As I show you the new skills that are going to be needed for remote work, it is important to remember that *as technology comes and goes, humanity does not.* I argue that being a decent human remains the most desirable and employable trait, right up there beside the all-important question, "*Can you deliver?*".

In case you are wondering, here are some essential universal actions I would consider to be a part of being a decent human in the workplace:

- Leading conversations with empathy
- Giving your full attention at the moment
- Using active listening rather than passive listening
- Making as much eye contact as possible during a conversation (*depending on the conversation medium, of course*)
- Not interrupting others during the conversation
- Saying "*thank you*" often
- Speaking clearly and in ways that are relatable to the end-user, customer, or client as much as possible

The ability to pick up the phone and talk to someone openly and honestly may have become a luxury item, but an even more luxurious and rare item is the ability to talk to a decent human being with great communication skills on the other end. This customer experience will only become more and more important as the planet grows increasingly remote and social skills continue to be neglected in school curriculum across the globe.

Recently, I hired a contractor from Slovenia to do some work for me. I was quite nervous as I had outsourced some contract work in the past and felt I didn't really get the value I paid for. However, I decided to take a chance on this person because he seemed like he could deliver and appeared to be a decent human being and a great communicator. For these reasons, I went with him.

Three months later, not only did he deliver amazing work for me on that job but we began building a mutually beneficial working relationship that remains intact today. We now partner in an affiliate business relationship and I recommend multiple clients to him each year. Why did I decide to do this? Because *I believe that great remote workers who deliver and who are decent humans deserve to be highlighted and rewarded as such.*

By entering into an affiliate partnership with this contractor, we both win. I get another stream of income (*a referral kickback*) and he acquires new clients without the added costs of advertising (*which equals more revenue for him*). Que Stephen Covey because this is a remote win/win!!

I share this example because *one of the new skills that is needed for remote work is going to be the ability to think outside the box and to be creative.* Rather than sticking to an existing revenue system that may work pretty well, being open to a new revenue system that may work even better and include decent people is going to give you a tremendous leg up in the remote working space. The cream always rises to the top, especially in remote settings. This skill is really about finding that cream and bringing it into your network more often.

#2 STAYING SELF-DISCIPLINED

Another skill that is going to continue to be needed for remote work well into the future is the age-old ability to be self-disciplined. There is always going to be work that you *want* to do and work that you *have* to do. Being able to discern the difference and to dance the line between urgent and important, between "this looks fun" and "this has to get done", will allow you to live a long and prosperous career of remote work. If the work that excites you is different from the work you may be waking up to on a Monday morning, it's important to remember that, just like life, we don't always get what we want. Sometimes your favorite candy is sold out. Sometimes it's going to rain before the sun shines. **Sometimes, your own agenda can't come first.**

The most important thing to remember here is that staying self-disciplined will keep you employable a lot longer than if you negate your discipline and always give in to the work that you want to do, rather than focusing first on what you NEED to do. This may seem simple but it's actually much harder to do than it sounds. It takes discipline and respecting the difference between "want to have" and "must-have." In a generation of learners graduating from a school system often void of strict deadlines and real accountability, this skill will become even harder and harder to identify when hiring remote workers.

#3 BUILDING BOUNDARIES

Another precondition to thrive in the 2020s while engaging in remote work is the ability to develop (*and adhere to*) clear-cut boundaries between your work and home life. In short, the ability to leave work tasks, projects, portfolios, and responsibilities at "work."

In the 2019 "State for Remote Work Report," 22% of remote workers indicated that they had a tough time unplugging after work.[16] While this number may actually be much larger in the 2020s as more folks transition into remote work, we have to be intentional in building and maintaining our remote working boundaries. Each and every job has its place and needs to be treated as so. No task, project, or position should consume you so much that you struggle to be present in your home and/or with your loved ones. While some countries have led the way in establishing work boundaries for their citizens (*thank you, France*) we cannot simply stand by and wait for our governments to do the same for you and me. **We need to create our own rules and clearly establish our own boundaries in order to thrive well into the future of remote work.**

I often find myself closing my laptop at the end of my workday with multiple unopened emails in my inbox. When I struggle to leave them unread, I recall something one of my mentors told me. When his phone would ring off the hook with clients needing "urgent" work done and I asked him why we weren't servicing all those calls he said to me, *"I do work that is either fast, cheap or accurate, and folks can choose any two of those options. If the work is really that urgent, it will be the first two but not accurate and I am in the business of being accurate."* He went on to teach me this important lesson that has become a laughable mantra at times:

What would people do if I were dead? This question puts things in perspective for me because all work at the time seems important, especially when you are so passionate about it, but does it really matter if you are dead? The company will move on and those emails will just be forwarded to someone else's inbox. Maybe the next time you feel you need to answer everything all the time, take a moment to reflect on what would happen if you were gone tomorrow. Doing so should help you close the laptop and be present with your loved ones. This may be a morbid way of thinking but sometimes we need to pull ourselves out of the clouds so that we can get more into reality.

Early in my career, I also decided that I would not put my work email on my phone unless it was mandated or the company I worked for was covering my phone bill in its entirety. This boundary alone has allowed me to be fully present in my home when my work ends for the day. It means I check my phone less and can be fully attentive with my family and in my life outside of work. This is my hope for you as well.

#4 STAYING SOCIAL

On a similar wavelength, the need for a solid social life is also going to be essential to thriving in the future of remote work.

Why?

Because loneliness and the ability to thrive do not pair well together.

Nothing is more emotionally satisfying than gathering together with a group of people (*in person, of course*) at the end of a workweek for a drink, workout, or catch up. Continuing to connect with your social circle and being intentional about connecting with them regularly is a sure way to improve your social-emotional health, mental health, and overall wellbeing as a remote worker.

During the winter of 2020, the organization I work for, like many others, went fully remote. Here I was, living in one of six cities in Canada with over one million people and I was rarely seeing anyone at all. After having an emotionally rough October of that year, I reached out to a friend (*who was new to working remotely*) and we started running together each week. We'd meet up in a parking lot on a Saturday morning, map out a route, throw the credit card in a pocket for a post-run coffee, and hit the road. We would talk about everything from marriage to our jobs to what we were planning to do during the week ahead. I would always leave these runs invigorated, full of joy and excitement that I was able to get active with a friend. I felt so grateful that we were able to connect, bond, and lift each other's spirits in preparation for the cold winter week ahead. Without these weekly interactions, I know that my remote thrivability would have decreased substantially.

The importance of staying social often seems obvious, but obvious is not always enough. We are social creatures by nature. Find one, two, or even three of your closest family members and/or friends, and start by intentionally connecting with them each week. This skill of intentional connection will allow you to thrive in your remote working environment and proactively avoid the creeping feelings of loneliness, isolation, and abandonment.

#5 THE ABILITY TO HYPERFOCUS

As I mentioned elsewhere, it is vital to hone your ability to remain focused in your remote working environment moving forward. While I would argue that activating this skill in all areas of our lives will produce thrivability benefits, let's first unpack this skill with respect to remote work.

Whether in traditional or remote office settings, you can tell when someone is focused or not. When someone is really focused, they tend to have a look about them that screams *"Don't interrupt me!"* that you can sense from their body language before you approach them. This level of focus is called "hyperfocus." Actively exercising hyperfocus is the reason why the rapid innovation noted in Chapter 1 exists and why authors can produce captivating books time and time again.

Near the end of *Star Wars: The Rise of Skywalker,* there is a scene in which Senator Palpatine has Jedi Rae pretty well defeated. Laying almost lifelessly on the ground, Jedi Rae looks up at the mass of ships falling from the sky, like fire bursting out of a volcano when she is suddenly able to look beyond the sea of destruction to the stars. Once focused on the stars, she begins to hear each individual Jedi whispering to her and urging her to continue her last-ditch effort to destroy Palpatine. At that moment, Rae was exhibiting the skill of hyperfocus; she was able to sift through the literal chaos to focus on the united voices that were motivating her to complete her mission to defeat Palpatine.

This level of focus is extremely rare in our non-fiction days, which are distraction-ridden at the best of times. However, if we can exhibit the ability to get to that level of focus, even for a few moments, day in and day out, we will produce tremendous results in our vocation.

So, how does one reach or cultivate this deep level of focus? Well, for one, you must find a trigger that can help facilitate a state of hyperfocus. For me, this involves listening to a YouTube channel of ambient or trance music, or even a good movie score such as any Christopher Nolan film soundtrack. To locate *your* trigger, you may involve experimenting with other forms of music or stimuli that can take you to a mental place where your focus is at an all-time high.

#6 CREATE SCIENCE EXPERIMENTS

As you continue your remote working journey as a professional, it is important to remember that you are the captain of your remote working vessel. While you steer the ship, however, you must also wear the scientist hat. If something isn't working, you need to adapt to ensure that it starts to work again. ***The ability to continually create small science experiments within your work is one of the greatest skills you can take into the future of remote work.*** Test new systems and try out new software. Sign up for a new subscription trial to use a new productivity tool. Try starting your day earlier and ending earlier. Test, test, test until you develop a formula that works for *you*. Maybe you work better with a different content management system, or maybe you don't. Either way, companies with employees who are willing to take those shots are more likely to continue succeeding over time.

In my work, I am all about conducting science experiments and testing new processes. One science experiment that has gone exceedingly well has been adopting a strategy called, "Context Scheduling."[17] When I first learned about this strategy, I was really struggling to manage my time. I was juggling seven projects along with helping my team plan a national event. I found myself exerting all my energy just trying to stay both caught up and away from my inbox at the same time. So, after reading an article posted on *Entrepreneur.com*, I decided I was going to pilot context scheduling for three weeks to see if it helped me better manage my time at work. Within days, I immediately felt better about my work, had more energy, and felt more accomplished than I had in months. It was an amazing feeling!

Fast forward to one year later, and this three-week science experiment is now a critical way of working for me. In fact, it has worked so well that my teammates began to take notice and now ⅓ of our team is using context scheduling, telling me how much it has improved the way they work and reduced their stress levels. This has led to increased employee engagement, employee satisfaction, and better overall energy management with agile remote projects.

If it weren't for testing out a new way of scheduling, ⅓ of our team (*including myself*) would still be floundering in our old ways, trying to effectively manage various projects. The point here is not to be afraid to test out or experiment with new strategies in your own work. Yes, the experiment could flop, but it could also be the next best thing for you, your colleagues, and your organization.

#7 IDEATION & EXECUTION

Remote workers who are able to conceive new ideas and execute on those ideas will take their companies to new heights in the 2020s and beyond. Being able to physically get into a room with a creative mind can yield creative results. However, with our lack of physical creativity space while remote, those who are able to bring creative thinking forward in remote settings will be those that continue to shape industry, enterprise, and society as a whole. ***Ideation + execution = progression, and that is what every company is looking for in these new working conditions.*** Can we make progress? Can we perform? Can we come up with new ideas? These questions keep so many business leaders up at night and they are in need of skilled, competent employees who can answer "*Yes!*" to each of these questions and make their company better.

If you can ideate and execute, it may be the greatest resume bullet that you can showcase in your next job interview. Do not underestimate these skills in exploring new remote positions. These two go hand in hand as top-tier employable skills. But if you can bring both to the table, you are in for a thriving career as a remote worker.

When these seven skills are actioned, they will not only allow you to thrive but also help you continue to stay ahead of the curve as your remote work evolves. In this next chapter, I want to talk about motivation over the long haul when it comes to your remote work. Remote work is a marathon, not a sprint, and motivation over the long run will take you further than the short adrenaline rush of a heart-pumping sprint ever could. It's time for you to manifest your marathon motivation.

Chapter 10

REMOTIVATION

"Most of us spend too much time on what is urgent and not enough time on what is important."
-Stephen Covey

How can you continue to stay motivated and engaged in your remote work over time?

With the future looking more and more remote, the way you celebrate milestones or professional accomplishments will continue to evolve, as well as how to stay motivated with your work. As traditional workspaces transform, we are forced to substitute blowing out the candles on a cake with colleagues for other ways of celebrating, like having a new french press delivered to your doorstep via Amazon.

One of the most overlooked areas of our professional lives is the ability to stop, take stock, and reflect on our accomplishments - both big and small. In more traditional office settings, achievements are often more visible. They come in the form of awards on a desk or framed certificates on the wall. They are gatherings in the conference room on a Friday afternoon to celebrate employee milestones and achievements. Even though engaging in collective celebrations is still possible virtually, this chapter is about how you can recognize your own achievements in remote settings.

While the "how" is still being navigated by many companies around the globe, I wanted to take a moment to remind you about the importance of not losing sight of celebrating individual wins, achievements, and successes. With loneliness becoming more and more of an epidemic (*especially for remote workers*) a great way to make folks feel more included is to actively acknowledge their achievements and successes throughout the year. **Every human thrives on appreciation and gratitude, and just because the conference room has switched to the Zoom room doesn't mean that celebrations should disappear.**

Now, maybe you are working in a job where honoring staff achievements isn't an intentional priority. If this is the case, here are some recommendations I have for finding ways to pump your own tires privately, regardless of how much or how well your employer chooses to recognize you in your remote setting.

JOURNALING

I have been journaling on and off for almost two decades, and its benefits are often revealed to me in a variety of ways throughout my life. Journaling can serve as a safe space to record your feelings and thoughts about the day, the week, or even the month. While our world seems to move faster and faster each day, the art of opening up your journal and exploring your feelings with a pen has never been more important for remote workers. If you find yourself feeling frustrated, burnt out, or even just a little "off", scanning through your journal can help reveal to you why that is. Within your journal, it should feel permissive to record your achievements and successes regularly. Think of it as the road map to your emotional self.

For me, journaling is more about understanding where I am in the universe and why my flame is lit (*or not lit*). For example, when I was teaching in the UAE, I journaled every day. When I reread those journal entries, I noticed that between October and May of that school year they became more negative and downtrodden. This gave me the emotional confidence that I needed to step away from that position as I did not like who I was becoming and where I was going emotionally within my job. My candle was being blown out each month and through journaling, or internal investigation, I finally understood that it was time to put my candle in a new place where it couldn't be stifled or blown out any longer.

For you, I would encourage building journaling into your routine - an idea I touched on when discussing the *energy amplifier blueprint*™ in Chapter 2. (*For even more on the benefits of journaling, reread Chapter 3.*) Do this for at least three weeks. **Keep it simple, keep it safe, and keep it raw.** Journaling with those three things in mind will give you what you need.

RECORDING MONTHLY MILESTONES

One superb strategy that I find keeps me motivated and excited with the remote work I do is writing out a series of monthly highlights in my journal. When I started doing this, it became a motivational game-changer. Each month I would write out all of the highlights that I was projecting to experience in the month ahead. Projections can be all work-related, home-related, or a blend of both as a remote worker. **The goal is to manifest highlights in your professional life each month.** Regardless of the emails, Google reviews, lack of recognition, and social media chatter, you are projecting highlights into reality and that is extremely powerful.

At the end of each month, I go back to my highlights list and check off each of the highlights that manifested in my life. At the same time, I also document highlights I didn't expect to experience and reflect on those I projected but didn't realize. This allows me to keep my candle burning each month in all aspects of my life so that I can continue to thrive in my remote work, within my home, and with my family. *This strategy is something I highly recommend, especially if you are finding yourself struggling with feelings of anxiety, loneliness, lack of direction, and/or stagnation.* Nothing can help you defeat those feelings more than having a series of twelve highlight reels on the year that you can carry with you moving forward.

Not only will these two strategies keep you engaged with your work, but they will also keep you motivated to continue to do great work in the future. I find the candle comparison to motivation as an interesting way to look at things. It takes minimal energy to get the candle lit (*strike a match or flick the lighter*) but, once lit, it can burn for hours, even days, without needing any additional energy. However, if a sudden breeze enters the room, the candle can blow out just as quickly as it was lit. This is motivation at its finest. Getting a few words of encouragement or affirmation from a colleague or your supervisor can light your candle for days or even weeks at a time. But, eventually, something else will flood into your work and snuff out your light, whether it's a bad customer review, a negative email, or negative feedback on your project that just went public. Any of these things, along with others I'm sure you're recalling right now, contribute to lower motivation, performance, and overall job satisfaction.

The challenging part of dealing with the wind that takes the motivation out of your sails in remote working environments is that you can no longer lean over your desk and talk to someone about it. Sure, you can talk to the plant on your desk or the dog lying at your feet but human-to-human validation of your feelings is not always accessible in this new way of working, as I'm sure many of you have come to realize. This is why strategies such as tracking milestones, quarterly goals, and recording your feelings in your journal are great ways to park emotions where they need to be parked while also being able to look back at your previous success roadmap for encouragement and motivation. In my own remote working experience, I have found this to be extremely helpful in avoiding the imposter syndrome rabbit hole discussed in Chapter 4 while keeping my candle continuously lit.

At the end of the day, tracking your own achievements, milestones, goals, and feelings will increase your capacity to thrive in remote working environments, regardless of what your employer chooses to acknowledge.

Having the tools to track your success internally will allow you to continue to feel the deep purpose behind why you do what you do professionally, and serve as a gentle reminder of the value you bring to your craft.

In the final chapter of this book, I want to leave you with some self-care thoughts and strategies as well as some additional ways you can continue to stay rejuvenated as a remote worker. Self-care is a foundational part of wellbeing and being able to say, "*no*" to inversely be able to say, "*yes*" to yourself and to your soul is a skill to be mastered, not merely explored.

Chapter 11

SELF-CARE

"Self-care is never a selfish act—it is simply good stewardship of the only gift I have, the gift I was put on earth to offer to others."
Parker J. Palmer

While this chapter could easily be an entire book in itself, I wanted to end this book by discussing self-care.

According to an article published on *PsychCentral*,

"Self-care is any activity that we do deliberately in order to take care of our mental, emotional, and physical health. Although it's a simple concept in theory, it's something we very often overlook. **Good self-care is key to improved mood and reduced anxiety. It's also key to a good relationship with oneself and others."*[18]

Another, more visual way of describing self-care, which I love, comes from Matthew McConaughey's book, *Greenlights*. In it, he says, *"Just because the seats are empty doesn't mean they're not taken. Sometimes the guest list needs to be for one. You."*[19]

While the routines, strategies, and resources mentioned in this book all support remote thrivability, *it is almost impossible to be well at work if we are not well in life.* These days, that can sometimes feel one and the same.

Creating habits that facilitate space for self-care for you and for your family should not be overlooked as you plan your days, weeks, and years of remote work. As you work to preserve your focus, attention, and ability to execute professionally, you cannot neglect your personal wellbeing and self-care needs along the way.

In my book *Your Best Decade*, I share many strategies and ideas that can help you create space for self-care in your life. For example, good self-care can start with saying "*no*" to the wrong things so that you can say "*yes*" to the right things.

Self-care is not selfish because it is about servicing your needs, not your desires. Good self-care involves navigating and sometimes eliminating negative relationships and influences from our lives. Good self-care also involves engaging in daily moderate to vigorous physical activity. It involves taking care of your body by eating healthy foods. These are just some of the ways that *Your Best Decade* can facilitate good awareness and action around self-care.

Another self-care idea I am seriously contemplating as a way to manage the unique stress and expectations involved in remote work is a life sabbatical. Similar to a retreat, this sabbatical takes the form of a restful, rejuvenating time away from technology. It is a season of intentionally stepping away from emails. It is relief from meetings and a time to recharge versus fight to meet deadlines. Sabbaticals are a great way to step back so that you can return to your work refreshed and renewed. While sabbaticals are typically associated with education professions, I believe that life sabbaticals need to be at least one month long, regardless of profession. In former President Barack Obama's book, *Promise Land*, he wrote about the sabbatical he and his family took immediately following his eight-year presidency, describing it as a season of relief, reconnection, and recalibration, which afforded him the space to start that book.

Although a life sabbatical may not always be feasible, it's never too early to start saving for a one to three-month fallow season away from remote work.[20] A sabbatical doesn't need to be expensive, either. Maybe you end up living in a van for two months. Maybe you rent out a cabin in the offseason for a month. There are tons of creative ways you can make life sabbaticals practical, affordable, and effective.

Additionally, there are some incredible self-care and soul-care strategies found in the book *Get Your Life Back: Everyday Practices For A World Gone Mad* by John Eldridge, which is listed in my book recommendations at the back of this book. The way John looks at the soul and rejuvenation is magnetic. It's worth a read if you want to dive deeper into self-care for your soul.

As we continue through our remote working adventure, I'm drawn back to the idea of creating science experiments. I have tested many different self-care strategies and routines throughout my life; at thirty, I began to really understand what works and what doesn't work for me. Having practiced self-care strategies for almost fifteen years, it has taken a long time to fully comprehend what I need (*and don't need*) to function well and optimally each day.

In navigating your own journey beyond the pages of this book, I encourage you to regularly conduct new science experiments regarding your self-care. Read new books, a lot. Try new activities, or carve out some time each year to reflect on your great days and dissect why they felt so great. Greatness leaves clues. Find them.

Looking back to look ahead is how we started this journey and it is only fitting that we end this part of the journey by looking back and thinking critically and intentionally about our self-care needs. Remind yourself that the goal in life is not more but *more depth* and your future self will thank you for it.

CONCLUSION

As I leave you to start (*or continue*) thriving in your remote working environments, I want to offer you some final words of encouragement.

By investing in this book alone, you have already taken a considerable step towards thriving in your remote working environment. But the journey does not stop here! Now is when the rubber meets the road. This book will close and your day-to-day responsibilities will carry on.

Moving forward, it will be a day in and day out grind to cultivate focused attention and meet your individual self-care needs all while juggling the various responsibilities and expectations that are a part of your life and vocation. **To thrive in remote working environments is a luxury and we must treat it as such.** Remote work comes with a range of privileges and challenges, but the opportunity to become the absolute best version of yourself remotely, while in the command center of your own home, is incredible! If our ancestors were still alive they would be salivating at the opportunities that we have in our lives today. Being able to build and maintain a career from home is a true blessing but it is up to you how much you allow that blessing to enrich your life.

Never before in human history have we been challenged to reach such a unique pinnacle of being by thriving in remote working environments.

It's up to you to accept the challenge and rise to the occasion!

NOTES

1. Huffington, A. (2019, December 27). *The best of 2019 and top trends for 2020: And here's to thriving in the new decade.* Thrive Global News. https://thriveglobal.com/stories/arianna-huffington-trends-burnout-leave-behind-new-year-outlook/

2. NASA Science. (2020, March 18). *Who has walked on the moon?* Solar System Exploration, NASA Science. https://solarsystem.nasa.gov/news/890/who-has-walked-on-the-moon/

3. Montag, A. (2018, May 24). *In 1985, Steve Jobs made these eerily accurate predictions about the future of tech.* CNBC Make It. https://www.cnbc.com/2018/05/24/apple-co-founder-steve-jobs-accurate-predictions-about-future-of-tech.html

4. Cafasso, J. (2018, September 18). *What is synaptic pruning?* Healthline. https://www.healthline.com/health/synaptic-pruning

5. Hoelzle, U. (2012, January). *The Google gospel of speed.* Think with Google. https://www.thinkwithgoogle.com/future-of-marketing/digital-transformation/the-google-gospel-of-speed-urs-hoelzle/

6. For more on Gary's work, visit https://www.garyvaynerchuk.com/

7. Dalla-Camina, M. (2018, September 3). *The reality of*

imposter syndrome: Feeling like an imposter? Know what it is and what to do about it. *Psychology Today*. Retrieved from https://www.psychologytoday.com/ca/blog/real-women/201809/the-reality-imposter-syndrome

8. Ravindran, S. (2016, November 15). *Feeling like a fraud: The impostor phenomenon in science writing*. The Open Notebook. https://www.theopennotebook.com/2016/11/15/feeling-like-a-fraud-the-impostor-phenomenon-in-science-writing/

9. Institute for Health and Human Potential. (2019). Emotional intelligence: The essential skill of the future-proofed workplace. Retrieved December 14, 2020 from https://www.ihhp.com/assets/EI-the-Skill-of-the-Future-Workplace.pdf

10. Institute for Health and Human Potential (2019). *The meaning of emotional intelligence.* Institute for Health and Human Potential. https://www.ihhp.com/meaning-of-emotional-intelligence/

11. McConaughey, M. (2020). *Greenlights*. Penguin Random House.

12. Canadian Society for Exercise Physiology. (2021). *Canadian 24-hour movement guidelines for adults ages 18-64 years: An integration of physical activity, sedentary behaviour, and sleep.* Canadian Society for Exercise Physiology. https://csepguidelines.ca/adults-18-64/

13. Lastoe, S. (n.d.). *This is nuts: It takes nearly 30 minutes to refocus after you get distracted.* The Muse. Retrieved January 24, 2021 from https://www.themuse.com/advice/this-is-nuts-it-takes-nearly-30-minutes-to-refocus-after-you-get-distracted#:~:text=But%20taking%20much%2Dneeded%20and,get%20back%20to%20the%20task.%E2%80%9D

14. Wiking, M. (2016). *The little book of hygge: The Danish way to live well.* Penguin Random House.

15. Marinova, I. (2020, November 21). *28 Need-to-know remote work statistics of 2020.* Review 42. https://review42.com/

remote-work-statistics/

16. Buffer. (2019). *State of remote work: How remote workers from around the world feel about remote work, the benefits and struggles that come along with it, and what it's like to be a remote worker in 2019*. Buffer. https://buffer.com/state-of-remote-work-2019#

17. Tank, A. (2020, February 25). *Take back your time with context scheduling*. Entrepreneur. https://www.entrepreneur.com/article/346589

18. Michael, R. (2016, August 10). *What self-care is -- and what it isn't*. PsychCentral. https://psychcentral.com/blog/what-self-care-is-and-what-it-isnt-2#1

19. McConaughey, M. (2020: 155). *Greenlights*. Penguin Random House.

20. *For more on fallow seasons, see:* Fahey, R. (2019, February 17). *Why we need to be 'ok' in the fallow season: How struggle can breed growth*. The Startup - Medium. https://medium.com/swlh/why-we-need-to-be-ok-in-the-fallow-season-1d049d4e6d05

21. Craig, L. (2018, September). *Are you suffering from imposter syndrome? Ways to identify and deal with feelings of self-doubt in grad school*. American Psychological Association. Retrieved November 15, 2020 from
https://www.apa.org/science/about/psa/2018/09/imposter-syndrome

BOOK RECOMMENDATIONS FOR REMOTE WORKERS

- » Remote - Jason Fried
- » Rework - Jason Fried
- » The Power of Habit - Charles Duhigg
- » Emotional Intelligence: Why It Can Matter More Than IQ - Daniel Goleman
- » Bringing Emotional Intelligence to the Workplace: Best Practices - Daniel Goleman
- » Deep Work: Rules for Focused Success in a Distracted World - Cal Newport
- » Digital Minimalism: Choosing a Focused Life in a Noisy World - Cal Newport
- » The 5AM Club - Robin Sharma
- » Mindset: The New Psychology of Success - Carol Dweck
- » Atomic Habits: An Easy & Proven Way to Build Good Habits & Break Bad Ones - James Clear
- » Get Your Life Back - John Eldridge
- » Limitless - Jim Kwik

www.ingramcontent.com/pod-product-compliance
Lightning Source LLC
Chambersburg PA
CBHW032039200426
43209CB00049B/36